Home Staging for Beginners

By Sophia Grace

Learn tips and tricks on how home staging can get you the top dollar when you sell your home!

2nd Edition

Table of Contents

Introduction

I want to thank you and congratulate you for purchasing the book, *"Home Staging for Beginners: Learn tips and tricks on how home staging can get you the top dollar when you sell your home"*.

This book contains proven steps and strategies on how to give your property a better image so that buyers will be enticed to purchase it as their new home.

It is obvious that money is a limited resource. Thus, we need to be meticulous whenever we need to buy something. This meticulousness is noticeable when it comes to purchasing objects that have higher value including real estate properties such as homes. This is why more people are now open to buying homes that were previously used rather than taking out a mortgage to build a new home. However, because the value of these "second hand properties" is still high, buyers exercise extreme caution during the selection process. Therefore, your goal as the seller is to research about methods that can help you get the attention of potential buyers so that they will consider your property.

This book will introduce to you some home staging techniques that you can employ in order to capture the interest of potential buyers of your property. The home staging techniques mentioned in this book also work in improving the value of your property.

Thanks again for purchasing this book, I hope you enjoy it!

Chapter 1 - Knowing the Basics of Home Staging

If selling products with small or average prices is quite a challenge, then it is safe to assume that you will find it even harder to sell something of great monetary value. One thing that fits this criterion is real estate property such as a house. However, it is still possible to sell your old home without having to reduce its price just to capture the interest of buyers. The secret lies in properly staging your home so that it gets the buyer's attention.

This chapter will discuss basic information about home staging.

What is home staging?

Many people are looking to have their own homes, and one option that they utilize in order to achieve this goal is to visit real estate listing sites for pre-owned properties. This is because listed properties are cheaper than taking out a mortgage for a brand new home; but even if your house is sold at a much lower price, this does not automatically assure that it will find a new owner. Even if buying pre-owned properties, buyers want make sure that they will get the best value for their money. Therefore, your goal is to get them to check out your house and see that what you offer to them is a property worth buying. This is where home staging comes in.

Home staging refers to the act of getting your private property ready for sale in the real estate market by making it appealing to prospect buyers. By transforming the look of your property so that it is more welcoming and attractive to the eyes of the buyers, you will have bigger chances of selling your property for the price that you desire. If you're lucky enough, you can even get the interest of more than one buyer, giving you an opportunity to offer the property to the buyer who can pay more than what others could give.

Before, home staging is not considered as an important factor to get your property sold. After all, it is common practice for home sellers to keep the property clean and presentable in order to entice buyers. However, in the year 2000, recession was experienced by many economies. This influenced buyers to implement strict guidelines when it comes to choosing what they buy, especially when looking to own a home. This led to the spread of home staging techniques to gain an edge over other properties that are posted for sale.

Why Do I Need to Stage My Home?

Many homeowners who are looking to sell their property think that staging their homes is simply a waste of time and money. Most of them think that they will never get back the resources that they put in home staging. Should you stage your home even though you are planning to put it on the market?

Home staging has always been an optional practice, but you will realize as you read on that it should not be the case. You have to think that you are making a very important financial transaction and you need to think through the process of selling your home. If you have sold a house before without staging your property, then you may have felt that you have sold it for less than its true value.

Real estate functions like a beauty pageant. There is always that big chance that there are other properties in your neighborhood or within 10 miles that are on sale when you listed your property. That means that you are not the only choice for buyers out there. When they see that your property is not ready to be moved in when they check it during the open house, they will surely move to the nearest open house that they see on the internet.

When buyers say that they need to pass on your offer because of a very visible flaw on your property, your house immediately serves as their standard for what they are not going to take. That means that they may not be coming back for a deed of sale.

Take a quick look at real estate with a seller's perspective – when you first acquired your house, you were very quick to notice all the quirks and the flaws, and you may have realized that it was too expensive for your means. You may also have realized that you would have to settle for another property because the house that you are selling does not work out for you anymore.

Now, look at your house from a buyer's perspective. Do you see it as a place of comfort, where you can spend time to improve your lifestyle? Do you see that your dreams are going to happen inside that house? Real estate is all about selling these dreams and plans. When you buy a house, you are making an emotional purchase.

For real estate experts, the money and time that you put in home staging is actually the reason why you allow your property to enter any real estate market that you are looking to sell to. Home staging provides you with the possibility of selling your property at a decent price, if not the price that you have in mind. It does not even matter what kind of market you are targeting. Without the leverage of having a presentable property to sell, you are going to not get any fair return on your investment. The time and money that you are going to invest to home staging make your property still worth the effort to sell.

If you are still not convinced, then here are some of the most important benefits that you will gain from home staging:

1. It makes you take the buyer's perspective.

You may think that any property buyer will fight for your piece of real estate, but it is best not to assume that that would be the case. You have to assume what a buyer will actually like in your house for him to shell out money or take a loan in exchange for your property. When you take the buyer's perspective, you will realize that there are many ways for you to improve your property, which can also help you raise its market price.

2. It makes you organize and de-clutter your belongings.

Having to sell your house means packing away your stuff, and you cannot find any other activity that gives you the head start to do this than home staging. When you stage your home, you will immediately see all the household items that you will not need in the house that you will be moving in to. At the same time, you can also avoid having to deal with packing your things in a hurry in any case a buyer comes along and wants to move in as soon as possible.

Staging also allows you to discover all the hidden flaws in your property and fix them ahead of time.

3. It makes you justify your price.

Face it – most buyers hire real estate agents that will make every move possible for you to lower your price. When you beautify your home and stage it just the way a customer wants it, you lessen the possibility of having to haggle over the price and even get better asking prices. While you may need to spend in order to stage your house, you will realize that making wise staging decisions can make you enjoy twice or thrice your investment. This activity places you in a great advantage since you are re-creating your home just the way buyers want it. Doing so will also make your customers trust you, thereby preventing them from asking too many unnecessary questions.

4. It lessens your property's time on the market.

Everyone who has opted to sell his or her property wants to make money out of it as soon as possible. If you have loans and you want to have an easier time moving in to your new property, you will definitely look for a real estate that will allow you to move as soon as possible. Beautiful homes always sell first, and home staging gives you that edge. When you stage your home, you can expect it to be out of your hands within the month, compared to un-staged houses that stay on listings for months, or even a few years.

How are home stagers different from interior decorators?

It can be quite confusing for some to differentiate between these two experts, primarily because the functions that they fulfill are the same (that is, they both focus on beautifying the home). However, the difference lies on the purpose as to why they make the property presentable.

Home stagers rearrange the look of your home to encourage other people to check out and eventually buy the property you are selling. Their job is to make a prospective buyer immediately think that your property can be their future home, instead of some run-in-the-mill real estate they can see in all buy and sell sites. Home stagers highlight certain facets of the home, so that buyers can see the potential beauty of the property if ever they start living there.

On the other hand, interior decorators rearrange the look of the home based on the preference of the homeowner so that it is appealing to them. This is similar to personalizing the look of your home. While both home stagers and interior decorators are knowledgeable on how to make your property look presentable, interior decorators are more concerned on how your property will appeal to you as their client.

Home stagers are very knowledgeable about the market, and they design and prepare your house with your buyers on mind. That makes them valuable when you are planning to increase your chances of moving your property fast on the market.

Will the value of my property increase with the help of home staging?

Once home staging is successful, you can expect the price of your property to increase. After all, your home will surely look differently than what it used to be. The number of people who will be interested to buy your property is also another factor that could dictate how much will be the increased on the price of your home.

On average, the selling price of staged homes can increase between 5 and 20%. This increase is significant enough to cover the services or equipment used for home staging, as well as to cover the depreciation of the property when it is not sold for a significant amount of time (so that it can be sold). With the increase of value and depreciation if not sold immediately, the amount that you can get once it's sold will somehow be higher or equal to the expected price of the property without staging.

How much will home staging cost?

The cost of home staging services depends on the number of areas in the house that needs refurbishing, as well as the floor area that needs staging. On average, the cost of home staging range from $500 to $5000, but if you are looking into making major repairs and renovations, you may have to spend a much bigger amount. However, before you scoff off at this spending budget, keep in mind that this price range is a smaller investment compared to how much money you can make out of a staged home!

Here is something that any professional home stager will tell you – all buyers are willing to spend $15000 on a staged home that is ready for moving in, rather than on a $5000 house that needs a lot of repairs and renovation. That means that you are bound to earn back double or triple the cost of your staging.

Do I need to hire professional home stagers?

Because of its importance when it comes to selling homes quickly, some individuals make home staging services their means of living. These people claim that home staging is more than simply cleaning your house so that it looks presentable. You also need to have knowledge about many home beautification methods in order to stage the best image for your home.

Because of extensive knowledge that home staging professionals possess, it is recommended that you contact them if you have the budget to pay for their service. This is because these professionals immediately see the changes needed by your property – something that you may not notice even if you are the former owner of the home. This is also recommended if you do not have much time to attend to the property being sold and make it presentable. Lastly, home stagers can give you an estimate for the price of the home once these are posted on property listings.

However, if you have knowledge and the time to stage the home you plan to sell, you can consider not hiring a professional home stager. While their skills are of big help, it is not necessary for you to contract their services in order to sell the property. This book will provide you numerous pointers on how you can stage your home just like a professional would.

Now that you know about home staging, you can start redecorating your old home so that buyers will be enticed to choose it over other properties.

Chapter 2 – How to Stage your Home, According to Brokers

When you are planning to stage your home, you may be thinking of hiring a professional to help you do the job. However, professional home stagers only have one advantage over you apart from their experience. They get advice from real estate brokers that tell them how houses should sell.

The Valuable Wisdom of Brokers

Brokers are the ones who can tell you how much your property probably costs when you put it out on the market. If you know a broker, he will surely tell you that staging your home can help you achieve the following:

1. Make buyers see your property as a future home

2. Walk through your property especially when they see it online

3. Positively affect the market value of your property when done according to your target's taste

Also, keep in mind that it will be extremely difficult to hire a real estate agent to help you move your property if you are not staging your home. The reason is simple – it is certainly difficult to sell an un-staged house. If you are going for a For Sale By Owner move and decide to sell your property by yourself, you will still need to stage it the way brokers and professional house stagers advise you to in order to avoid any problems in selling.

Be prepared to spend money for home staging

Even if you will not contract the services of a home stager, you will need to spend money in order for the process to be successful. At this point, you need to keep in mind that buying or renting staging props may become inevitable, and you need to repair or hide all the wear and tear that the years have brought upon your property.

Do not worry about the expenses – all real estate experts can attest that every owner who considered selling his or her property can earn double or triple the money spent for staging. Take note that even the ideas that you get from Pinterest still means spending. If it means that you need to spend thousands of dollars on your property to move it, then do so. Keep in mind that there are thousands of properties available out there, and making your home look and feel valuable and pristine will be an important advantage.

Top 10 Broker's Advice to Spending for Staging

Before you even think of staging your home, you have to keep in mind that you also need to think like a broker, whose job is to sell your property. What does every broker advice to homeowners who are looking to improve the asking price of their property and sell it quickly? Here are 10 of their most useful tips that will also prepare you for staging:

1. Make your house look roomy

If you have invested in a non-structural wall or a kitchen island, remove them. Anything that tells that your house has more space and wide floor plan says that it is easy to move in the market.

If you do not have enough floor area in your home, you may want to opt for a minimalist approach to staging. That means that you may want to remove as much furniture as possible.

2. Take away anything in your yard that blocks the sight.

Most homeowners forget to trim trees and when you are looking to sell your house, see to it that you add landscaping to your budget. By improving your landscape, you ensure that your property stands out and has a curb appeal that will definitely attract buyers in the neighborhood who are looking for listed properties. According to a survey conducted by HomeGain, spending about $500 for landscape can bring you a return of $2000 once you are able to sell your house.

3. Make sure that you bring in light.

Houses that have ample lighting are very valuable, and that is because lighting sets the mood of the buyer during the open house. When you plan to stage your home, take the time to invest in sun tubes and skylights when you know that you need natural light to make the rooms feel larger. You also need lights to bring warmth to empty spaces. Also, invest in a good balance of high wattage and soft light bulbs.

Brokers also advise sellers to keep all lights on during the open house, even during daytime. The reason is that most buyers do not like checking areas with poor lighting, and that may lead to making them skip an area that is a potential selling point.

4. Maintenance is a must.

Many homeowners think that whoever will take their house can look past the flaws and fix broken facilities themselves. However, leaks, insulation problems, and broken panels can easily turn off any buyer. Simply seeing to it that you spend a few hundred dollars on these things will put in additional thousands of dollars to your home's value.

5. Green efficiency is the way to earn greenbacks.

Invest in energy efficient appliances and make your roofing and insulation efficient as well, so the potential buyers will appreciate your effort of maintaining the good condition and efficiency of your property. There are a lot of appraisers out there who do not figure this yet, but buyers today are willing to put a lot of money for cost saving. You can also expect your buyers to ask for utilities, which is a new trend in real estate that will go on in the future.

6. The front door is a mind-bending tool.

Do not ever underestimate what your front door can do for your home's value. Most buyers make up their minds during the first seconds of entering properties, and will keep on looking for reasons to support their decision when they tour a home. If your prospective buyers will not consider your front door worth entering, then you are missing out on a sale.

7. Invest on your floors.

Ninety-four percent of real estate experts recommend spending at least $600 on floor renovation, and that money is going to be spent well because you can expect up to $2000 return when you were able to sell your property. There is also a good chance that you are going to spend less if you are looking for minor repair projects, such as nailing in a squeaky board or replacing a broken tile. However, do not let your floors clash with all the upgrades that you are looking to do in your property. Neglecting to upgrade them as well will make them noticeable and dissuade buyers from considering your house.

8. Spend for the bathroom.

All brokers recommend that you should make major improvements in tiled areas like the kitchen and bathroom. However, you have to prepare yourself – these areas can be very costly.

Do not lose hope yet – spending $500 for the bathroom can positively improve the area. People are paying extra consideration for the bathroom since it is the second most-visited area in the household, and therefore there is a great chance that they will buy your property when you have this area tuned up.

9. Spend for the paint job.

If the home features extreme colors such as purple or orange, you will need to replace them with neutral colors. You may need to allocate a significant amount of money in order for your walls and floors to be repainted or replaced with a less distracting shade.

10. Spend for eliminating all the "What's that?" possibilities.

Take the time to spot all the fixtures and items in your house that may introduce unwanted "curiosities", such as wallpapers that lie about the age and value of your property, moldy antiques, and outdated appliances. It is worth your money to fix or replace them – the more questions buyers ask, the less likely they will buy.

Although you can expect to spend a small amount of money to stage your home (in order to buy accessories and do some repairs), there are certain situations wherein you will need to dole out a bigger amount. These situations are the following:

- If the amount of the property you are selling is quite huge, you need to make sure that what is inside it is not outdated. By sticking with your old-looking and outdated furniture or appliance, buyers may think that you are asking for too much. The solution would be to rent upscale appliance or furniture, even for a few months (until the property is sold). This could cost you quite a lot, but this is a much cheaper alternative than buying new furniture.

- You may also look into shopping for staging props if you are hesitant to rent furniture or lend your appliances to the open house. Yes, you can add furniture and appliances during the home staging process in order to suggest to buyers how they may want to place their stuff right after they moved in and display how their lives may look like once they manage to move in.

- Storage space rental is necessary if you are to remove the furniture or objects that you do not want your buyers to see. It is ill advised to use one of the rooms at the home you are trying to sell as storage, as you want buyers to see the full potential of your property. It is also safer, as buyers will not have access to your personal belongings.

Chapter 3 – Getting on with Home Staging

In the previous chapter, it was mentioned that it is not required for you to hire a home stager in order to improve the look of your house and sell it quickly; but what should you do in order to get your home staged without hiring a professional?

This chapter will provide you with the basics of home staging preparation if you plan to do it without professional help.

Preparing for home staging

Before you actually start modifying the look of your property, you need to do the following preparations:

Know who will be your potential buyers

Your home staging efforts will produce better results if you have an idea as to the types of buyers that you may encounter. This will help you in designing your home in a way that appeals to these buyers. For example, if most of the buyers are on a specific age group or gender, the look of your house should be able to capture their interest. Are they single males who are looking for a place close to workplace? Maybe they are more interested in buying your property if it looks like a man cave. Are you looking to sell to a young family who wants their children in a suburban community? Maybe you should dress up your house with rustic furniture.

You can deal with all these concerns by asking real estate agents regarding the demography of buyers looking for a home in your area. You can also look online for websites that display the demography of households in your neighborhood. Take note that people are more willing to adapt to the environment that they are moving into, so make sure that you are dressing up your property in such a way that anyone can distinguish it from all the houses on sale in your area.

Think of the home as your investment, not a place that you want to stay at

The purpose of home staging is to "depersonalize" the home. This simply means that the look of your property should be neutral enough so that buyers can imagine themselves living inside it. Therefore, you need to think that the home is not yours, and that its design should not be aimed towards getting your attention. By getting too attached with your home and having it look like how you want it to be, the property may not get sold right away (since the property seems to be "too personalized" for the buyer).

You may expect yourself to get emotionally attached to all the features that you might need to let go – it is just normal, considering that you broke your back and spent a small fortune making your property look like how it was before you decided to sell it. However, your idea of perfection may not apply to the next person who is going to live on it. If you believe that that teal paint on the bedroom makes a lot of sense because it makes your duvet look great, ask yourself if the next owner has the same duvet as yours. The chances are very slim. Now you know why you need to repaint.

One good way to accomplish this goal is to remove items that will make it look like a personal space, such as photos of you and your family, or the awards framed and hanged on the walls. If you particularly like that chandelier in the living room, but all your guests say that it clashes with the walls, then remove it. Take note that what may seem great for you may seem awful for others, and that means that you need to take the minimalist approach when you are trying to stage your house. This will let you stay on the safe side.

Work with your Real Estate Agent

If you are not willing to hire a professional home stager, you should at least consult a real estate agent to help you appraise the value of your property and get valuable tips on how you can improve any buyer's asking price. Your real estate agent will be more than happy to help you when it comes to staging your home. Improving your home's value helps him move your property faster, which will eventually let him earn a commission.

Real estate agents are famous for working closely with professional home stagers and they are knowledgeable in pointing out all the possible flaws in your property that may dissuade buyers from even touring your home. They can also tell you the best market for the kind of property that you own, and knowing that information gives you an idea on how you should improve your house in order to attract a specific niche market.

If you are gunning for a FSBO (for sale by owner) selling, then you may need to do more research about your market and the staging style that you need to apply to your home. Here is a tip for those who are looking to save the commission for themselves: visit the best home that you know in your neighborhood and try to make your property look similar to that property as much as possible. The reason is that most future homeowners do not want their new house to stick out too much from the rest of the houses near them.

Most of them want one that seems like the most coveted property in the neighborhood they are moving into.

Prepare a To-Do List

Now that you have your intentions clear about staging your home and have a list of tips coming from your agent on how you can improve the chances of getting your property sold, prepare to organize your thoughts. Set your ideas on paper and commit to them. Remember that you are also on the mission of staging your house in the most cost-efficient way, and creating a to-do list can help you cover all the areas in your house that you need to dress up without the mistake of buying too much props or paint that you cannot use after this project.

Before you set on home staging, prepare a detailed itinerary on what you should spend for (you can refer to the previous chapter for this) and what times should you be tending to the different areas of your house. That will give your agent the heads up on when he can list your house for sale. Your to-do list should also contain all the spots in your house that you need to pay extra attention to, such as dated tiles and cabinets, attic insulation and furniture update, along with the most efficient solutions you can come up with. You should still be able to make any changes to this to-do list as you go, but being prepared will enable you to stage your house in less time than doing this project without any aim.

Now, you are ready to tackle that property and convert it into the dream house that everybody would love to buy!

Chapter 4 – Things You Need to Do Before Decorating

After doing the necessary preparations, you can now start applying the basic steps needed to stage your home. These steps are the most important ones that will lead you into discovering all the other steps that you need to take in order to make buyers become interested in your property.

While staging means having to change the way your property looks in order to make it more attractive, it also means going back to the basics, such as cleaning and organizing your house and seeing to it that every switch and faucet are working properly. You need to see through all these things before getting to the creative process of designing your home – think that all buyers want a functional property before they even think of living in it.

This chapter will help you take care of most of the questions about your property before buyers even get to ask them.

De-clutter your home

Most buyers like the idea of being the first inhabitants of a property that they saw on sale. They may have the idea that you lived in it before, but they will definitely want to buy it when it does not have the lived-in look. That means that you need to let go of your clutter.

It is a common trend to see staged homes sell within a month, while un-staged ones stay in the market for three to four months. That means to say that if you have decided to stage your home, then you will need to pack and move elsewhere. The moment your home gets listed, there's a big chance that it gets sold right away.

De-cluttering your home before you list it on sale is important. First, you need to consider that unorganized belongings hide selling points in your house – if buyer's can't see them, then you lose all the possible edges that you already have in selling your home. Second, de-cluttering and organizing your stuff also allows you to keep track of all the things that you have and should go to your new house. That reduces the chances of having to pack in panic when a buyer comes in and takes your house earlier than you have expected.

If you as the homeowner do not want to see unimportant stuff in your house, this is very true for those who are looking to buy a home. Of course, it is an obvious fact that we want our surroundings to be free from unnecessary objects. Therefore, your first step for cleaning and beautifying the property is to remove clutter. This is one of the major things that can improve the image you want to project to buyers once they visit your property. By removing clutter, your home will most likely end up with more space. In more ways than you can imagine, this can make your home look more appealing.

In deciding which objects you should consider as clutter, remember to stick to the essentials of the home. Make sure that the things displayed in your property are enough for you to live comfortably. Minimalism will give the impression that your house is spacious and that the buyer will have enough room to personalize that home.

For example, if you previously have a long table that can accommodate eight people in your dining room, you can consider renting a good-looking but smaller dining table enough for 4 to 6 diners. Remember the 80-20 rule; that is, only 20% of all your belongings are used 80% of the time. Therefore, objects that you do not use that often should be removed from your property.

Your goal is to sell the space that your home could provide – not the things inside it. Thus, your focus should be to highlight the available space that the buyer can use in your home.

Clean your entire home!

Here's where most homeowners and real estate agents fail – they do not clean the property that they are trying to move in the market. Since staging is all about selling the idea that a property is worth living in, a dirty house translates to an unsold house.

If you are thinking that it is the buyer's responsibility to clean up your house when they move in, then you are wrong. Buyers actually prefer a clean house and when you are preparing to hand over the keys to your front door, you should think that no one wants to deal with the extra hassle of having to clean a newly acquired property. A dirty house raises many questions, and these questions point to your reputation.

You have to be careful before you ask your agent to list your property and open it for tours. Some prospective buyers really take the time to leave a comment in online realty sites, and a bad comment on your property will only delay a possible sale.

Aside from removing unnecessary junk, make sure that your property is clean wherever you look. By keeping it spotlessly clean, you are adding beauty to the property and somehow tells your customers that it is a nice place to stay. Additionally, nobody wants to live in a house that looks messy and lacks maintenance.

Cleaning should be thorough. Some buyers are meticulous, and they may back out at the first sign of dirt on even the smallest area in your house. Of course, cleaning should be done both inside and outside the house. Apply every cleaning technique (sweeping, mowing the lawn, vacuuming, or fumigating) that you could think of, so that buyers will see the property as flawless. Maintain the cleanliness of the house regularly, as you do not know when visitors will decide to check on your property.

Update Anything that Concerns Electricity

Buyers are very concerned about utilities, and among the first things that they will most likely touch in your house is the light switch. You can also expect them to ask you how many electrical sockets are there and which ones are working. These things are major concerns and in order to get these out of the way, ask an electrician to see your property's wiring. It is also the best time to change the switch covers and panels while you have a professional working with you for electrical concerns.

Another great idea is to start adding or removing electric sockets and lighting fixtures in your rooms before you decorating them. If you are planning to turn a bedroom into a home studio to appeal to artists, then you may want to improve the lighting and add a couple of wall sockets.

Apart from updating your electrical wiring, you can also make other renovations that you think are appealing to prospective buyers. However, keep in mind that you should not go over the top. The next chapter will tell you more about changes that you need to avoid.

Chapter 5 – Things You Should Avoid Doing

Now that you are updating your home in order to make it more valuable to buyers, you should take care not to accidentally devalue your property before you put it out on sale.

Many homeowners make expensive last-minute home improvement projects with the hopes that it will make their properties thousands of dollars more expensive than the original value. However, these homeowners are not aware that doing so can seriously hurt their houses' value and make them stay in the market longer than usual.

Here are the top home improvement projects that you need to avoid when you are looking into staging your home and making some changes to its layout before setting it up for a sale show.

1. Extreme Kitchen Renovations

If you think that a $15000 kitchen upgrade will improve your house's value on the market and will attract the rich and the famous into buying your property, you could be sending that money down the drain. One of the well-known turnoffs for buyers is the over-the-top kitchen, especially if you are targeting a wider market in order to sell your home quickly.

Avoid staging your home with restaurant-type stoves and kitchen islands. In addition, steer clear from multiple refrigerators. Your buyer will add them if their households need them.

2. Hot Tubs and Pools

Adding a pool and a hot tub may significantly increase your home's value to about 11%, but you have to be careful. There are too many buyers out there who think that they do not need extra swimming and maintenance costs, which may mean additional $3000 yearly expense on their household. Some buyers also think that having a pool is a safety liability, especially if they are moving in with children. Pools and hot tubs may also hurt your homeowner's insurance coverage and limit the number of people that your property can accommodate.

3. Specialty Rooms

Many homeowners love tearing off walls in order to create amenities that will serve their personal interests. However, if you are thinking of converting your garage into a gym or a mini basketball court, hold that thought. You may be dissuading potential buyers from looking into your property because you just took away the area where they could park their car.

4. Lessening the Number of Bedrooms

If you had torn down a wall adjoining the master's bedroom and the smaller room next to it, you might want to consider putting it back again before you list your home for sale. Homebuyers are very particular about the presumed number of rooms available in the property and if you have converted your originally 4-bedroom apartment into a 2-bedroom because you want bigger rooms, you might have shaved off thousands of dollars from your property's value.

5. Lessening the Number of Toilets

Here is another thing that you need to remember – never convert toilets into storage facilities, especially the bathroom downstairs. Buyers are very particular when it comes to bathrooms and the more you have, the better the price of your property. However, avoid the idea of adding an additional bathroom if that will only make your home's original layout suffer.

6. Unattractive Features

If you have installed a tacky painting on the wall or have added a very unattractive water fountain in your garden, then you might want to take them away. You might also want to hide satellite dishes that are too visible. These features can seriously distract buyers from seeing your home's more attractive sights, or even make them think that the square footing of your property is too small than what you have mentioned in your property's listing.

Take note that renovating your home before placing it on sale has pros and cons, and should you need to do some updates in order to increase its value, you will need to consider the buyer's perspective. It is also best to consult your broker before you make any irreparable damage to your property's value and get a pricing result that you want to avoid.

Chapter 6 - Specific Home Staging Tips for Different Areas in Your Property

While the previous chapter enumerated the home staging tips that you should follow all over the house, it did not focus on any particular area. Sure, the general look of the property can influence your customers to consider buying your home. However, the final decision as to whether the property is sold immediately lies on how the specific areas in the home will be staged.

This chapter will provide you with home staging techniques that you should apply for each area of the property that you are looking to sell.

Assume the visitor's perspective

How would you be able to find out which areas need more work and which features need to be highlighted? The way to answer that question is to think that you are looking at your home for the first time. Forget that you are the owner – think that you are a visitor in an open house.

Re-enter your home and stand in the doorway. Survey your entire house from this point – which areas are getting your attention in a bad way? Which of your home's features make you think that you are going to sell your house quickly if buyers can see them quickly? When you are able to spot the good and the bad in your house quickly, there's a good chance that buyers who would enter your house can spot them too. Go from room to room and list these features down.

How to prep your home's exterior

The first area that you would have to focus on for home staging should be the outside of your home. This serves as your "welcome message" to visitors, as what they see could influence their decision of continuing to enter your property and look inside (after all, first impressions last). Take the shoes of the customer and cross the street to look at your home. If your home has that curb appeal, then you have a great chance of getting it sold!

Here are some tips from real estate agents and home stagers that you can take to make your front yard (and eventually your home) more appealing:

- If the house is almost invisible because of the trees, grasses, or hedges around it, consider trimming these areas. Make sure that if you take a photo of the property, the abovementioned areas serve as the frame of your home. Maintain a uniform shape for your hedge, and get help from expert tree cutters to bring down branches that may be covering your home. You may need to spend $10 to $100 to do this, but you will also get a return of 100-200%.

- Consider the exterior paint of your home, making sure that it is limited to two or three shades only. Unfortunately, having too many shades for your home do not necessarily appeal to most buyers. If the property's area is quite huge, repainting will be a huge expense and may not be possible. What you can do is to get the exterior clean enough to entice the potential buyer. You can do this by using a pressure washer around the house, most especially on the walkways and the window shutters.

- Check out the roof and look for moss or dry rot on your gutter. Make sure that they are not broken, and that it can properly catch and remove rainwater.

- Keep garbage cans away from where the buyer can see them. Take your trash bag to the dump immediately to prevent your property from getting a bad smell and projecting a negative image to your potential buyers.

- Add color to your property by placing flowers or shrubs around it. Even artificial flowers can do the job of beautifying your property. This is done not only to avoid spending too much, but also to eliminate the need for checking every plant box or hedge for wilted leaves or petals. You can also leave artificial flowers outside to make it look appealing. You can also consider putting real flowers planted in pots, as they give the same appeal as those directly planted in your lawn or garden.

- Make sure that your lawn is raked, mowed, and thoroughly cleaned. Remove any foreign object such as children's toys or even stuff left by your pets (such as bones, fetch balls, and even litter!). If the grass on your lawn is not well-tended and looks withered, you can consider using non-toxic spray paints to make it look more alive. This technique is used in many golf courses to cover brown spots. On the other hand, if your lawn is in a bad condition, consider re-sodding it as early as you can.

- Consider accessorizing the outside of your home. This will give potential buyers an idea as to what they can do if they want to stay outdoors. You can place a grill, hammock, or outdoor furniture that is sturdy enough to resist the elements even when left outside. You also have to make sure that welcome mats, although considered as rags, should be presentable. If you have a patio with ample space, place a bistro table there, along with a couple of comfortable chairs.

- If your lawn or garden has a sprinkler, make sure that they are working. If the potential buyers visit during the morning or afternoon and the weather is fine, you can operate the sprinkler for a short period of time.

- Make sure that the door to the home is painted with a more attractive and brighter color than the rest of the property. This serves as an invitation for buyers to come in and check out what you are selling.

- Your driveway is one of the most important selling points of your house, so make sure to spend some time and effort in highlighting it. If you have a paved driveway, you may want to add a coat of sealer to make it look sleeker to buyers. If your driveway is made of gravel, then install stamped concrete or make use of interlocking stone. You will get up to 75% back on what you are going to spend for your driveway and 100%

edge over a neighbor who is trying to sell their house as well.

- Put a lot of attention to your front door – Repaint it or replace it if needed. If you do not have any roofing above the main door and you know that fumbling for keys during the rainy season is a sure way to get drenched, then extend your roof over this spot.

Set up your living room

The living room is often used as the entertainment center of most households. It is also the most commonly used area in the house, so make sure that you put a lot of attention to this room. Here are some tips to make your living room welcoming:

- Remove most of the picture frames, trophies or medals in this area, but see to it that you leave some of the most generic-looking ones in order to give an idea about the perfect place to add photographs and similar items.

- Deep clean your sofa. Use a neutral-colored slipcover and throw pillows to soften the mood.

- Stow away all your office equipment if you were fond of using this area for work. While office desks and books may seem functional, they may not appeal to buyers who are going to check out your home.

How to get your kitchen ready for cooking and viewing

The general home staging tips mentioned in the previous section are applicable for most of the rooms inside your home, especially the areas where people usually stay (such as the living and dining room; but aside from these general tips, another area that needs specific home staging techniques aside from the property's exterior is the kitchen.

Keep in mind that a staged kitchen is not necessarily a practical kitchen. A staged kitchen should be able to show potential buyers the following:

1. That your kitchen smells, feels and looks fresh and clean

2. That your kitchen is good looking and tasteful, and simple enough to make room for some personal changes later on

3. That your kitchen is welcoming and easy for other people to imagine spending time in there

4. That there are signs of activity and life there without being messy

If you do not know how to improve the look of this area, you can apply the following techniques:

- Make sure that the countertop is thoroughly clean and only contains few necessary items such as condiments. This will give the buyer an idea as to how much working space will be available for them when cooking. Consider placing accessories such as basket of fruits to make it look enticing.

- Wash and sweep the floors to get rid of stains or dropped ingredients used while cooking.

- Since the kitchen needs the faucet, make sure that it is working properly. If water is dripping from the faucet, replace it immediately. Likewise, check your sink so that it looks presentable. Also, check the plumbing so that drained liquids will not drip and flood the area.

- Check if the items inside your cabinets are organized. This also includes the cabinet where the drainage for your sink is hidden. If ever the cabinet doors are broken, repair them at once. Some customers would also like to check how much space could be stored inside the cabinet. If you are thinking that you can hide the clutter in your cupboard and kitchen cabinets, you are wrong. Hide all the extra stuff and mismatched items from sight, or take them out of your property to be safe.

- Many people have the habit of attaching mail and reminders on the refrigerator or any other appliance in the kitchen. Make sure that these documents are put away so that your privacy is protected.

- Make sure that your pantry is clean. Being the storage room for food, having an unorganized pantry might convey the message that pests such as cockroaches or rats may be infesting the property.

- Be extra sensitive to smell. A smelly kitchen means a dirty kitchen, and that means that you need to clean your garbage cans and disinfect the entire room. It is also wise to keep your pets elsewhere, if you have any.

- If you have a broom closet, make sure that everything inside is organized as well.

- Set the table for dinner in order to set the mood. That will make buyers see how the dining room can be prepared when they move in.

Bathroom home staging techniques

Another area in your home that, when properly staged, can make the buyers decide if the property should be bought or not is the bathroom. After all, nobody wants to live at a bathroom that looks unpleasant and disgusting.

The following are some of the techniques that you can apply in order to stage your bathroom properly:

- Make sure that no dirty towels and clothes are visible once the visitor enters the bathroom. This could give them the idea that the whole bathroom is dirty. It would also help if you place new and more attractive-looking towels, as it conveys the image that the area is thoroughly clean.

  Here is another tip: make use of white bathroom towels and stage the bathroom with white accessories. White can give the impression that your bathroom is cleaner and bigger than it actually is.

- If your bathroom is too small and you want to create the illusion that it is bigger, then install more mirrors. If you want to update the mirrors that are already installed, you can consider framing them in order for them to have that elegant look.

- Make sure that the parts of your bathroom are working properly. This includes the faucet and sink, the bathtub, and the toilet. If you have water heater installed on your shower, make sure that it will not cause electrocution. Also, see to it that other parts of the bathroom will not cause injuries (putting mats on areas that may be slippery, or replacing broken tiles that may collapse anytime and get you wounded).

- Make sure that the whole bathroom is spotlessly clean. Markings from water droplets may be evident on the walls if the area is not thoroughly cleaned. The same is true if you have mirrors inside the bathroom. The floors should also be washed and dried.

  Also, replace shower curtains and everything wherein molds secretly hide. Remember that all visitors and buyers can be more discerning and in tune with dirt and may easily spot all the dirt that you are trying to mask in this area.

- Remove all the clutter in the bathroom, including all the contents of your medicine cabinet, scattered makeup and soap bars. You can accessorize your bathroom by placing colorful soaps or hand wash gels.

Setting up your bedroom

Aside from the living room, another area in the home where people usually stay for a significant amount of time is the bedroom. Note that it is also an area in your property that most buyers want to personalize once they move in. Therefore, it needs to be enticing enough so that the buyers can see themselves resting on your property as their new home.

The techniques mentioned below can be followed in order to stage your bedroom so that it looks good and more relaxing:

- Make sure that there are no dirty clothes on your hooks, hamper, and the floor. You also have to remove unnecessary stuff inside your dressers, as well as organize what is inside it. Keep in mind that your buyers will take a look at all cabinets and drawers to check how they are going to organize their belongings there, so make sure that you take out your personal items.

- Make sure that the beds are made and that it should have fresh sheets. Plump your pillows to look more enticing. Make use of linens in neutral colors when you are staging your bed.

- Sweep the floors regularly or vacuum your rugs and/or carpets. If rugs or carpets are damaged (such as if there are dents), you can choose to replace it with a new rug or "heal" it so that it looks good. This is possible by using ice cubes on the areas where the carpet is damaged. Once the ice is melted and dried, the dents will be removed due to the fibers of the carpet being lifted up.

- Consider removing extra furniture from the bedroom, leaving only the bedside table, a dresser and the bed to allow more walking space. Also, make sure that you have a full-length mirror in the room to make the space seem larger.

- Make sure that the room's paint has a "cooler" shade. This is important so that the buyer will be more enticed to relax. Spruce up the room with an art piece or two to tell something about your taste as well.

Odd numbers work wonders when accessorizing your property

Even if it was mentioned that clutter and unused stuff should be removed from your home, it does not mean that you should also remove all aesthetically appealing items. What we are trying to say is that you should keep the accessories to a minimum, so that the buyer will be focused on the space. However, how can you say that your property's accessories are stripped to its bare minimum? Make sure that it is an odd number, preferably three. For example, it is pleasing to see a living room table that has three candles, or a differently shaded curtain in the middle of two similar designs.

For this accessorizing tip to be more effective, make sure that the accessories follow a "triangle" pattern. Place the items on each of these points. Also, consider the available space and the size of your accessories, making sure that they are properly distributed to prevent it from looking overcrowded. If the sizes vary, make sure that the smallest is placed in front and the largest is at the back. You can also consider grouping the accessories to make them more appealing.

By following the basics for home staging, you are moving one step closer towards getting your home sold faster and for a better price. Make sure that each of the guidelines mentioned above are applied in all areas of your home.

Chapter 7 – Things to Do During Open House

Now that you have managed to stage all the rooms in your house, you are now ready to welcome buyers. When you have already listed your property, it means that you can start expecting potential buyers to contact you or your agent to see how it looks like.

Even when you have already staged your house, you need to be sure that nothing will go wrong during your big presentation. Here are some tips that most stagers and real estate experts give to people who are looking to attract the right buyers and get the best asking price during an open house.

Use Technology to your Advantage

If you are looking to hold an open house soon, use an app to make it easier for you to invite prospective buyers into your property. Keep in mind that most buyers nowadays scour the Internet for properties and if you want to be found first, you need to use the web to your advantage. If you are selling your property on your own, you can use popular realty sites such as Zillow.com and Trulia.com. Realtor.com also offers an app to buyers to enable them to see properties for sale within a specific radius. The site even offers maps to help them reach listed houses easily.

Use Signs to Increase Foot Traffic

If you want to save money and paper, but still invite possible consumers to your open house, place a sign in your yard that is visible across the street. It would be a good idea to place that sign exactly one week before your big day in order for them to prepare and inform their real estate agents that they are eyeing your property.

Ask your Neighbors to Cooperate

Your neighbors can be a big factor when it comes to selling your house. You can expect them to be among the most important allies in spreading the word about your sale, or become the nuisance that will drive buyers away. Before you have an open house, inform them about your big event and tell them something about your property. Doing so will lessen the chances of having to combat the neighbor's noise. At the same time, inviting them to your open house will also widen your network.

Leave the House if you Have an Agent

If you plan to hire an agent to show your property during the open house, you do not need to be there. The reason is simple – it makes harder for buyers to see themselves as the owner of the house when you are around. It also makes it harder for them to ask questions and make comments about the property when they do not have anonymity.

If you are selling on your own, then refrain from telling potential buyers too much about your recent updates and home's features – they will figure it out on their own and raise questions when needed. Let them freely roam the property to make up their minds whether they will get the property or keep looking.

Make sure that your property is lighted for the duration of sale hours

The idea of house staging is to let the buyers see the potential of the whole house, starting from the yard up until the last room in it. To show the true beauty of the property though, you need to have it lighted. This is also one technique to make the rooms or the inside of the house look bigger.

It is advisable to use as much sunlight as possible. Not only will it help prevent getting a huge electricity bill, it could also create the impression that your property has a good ambiance. Open the windows and remove all window accessories (such as curtains or blinds), as long as your walls do not have any obvious holes or visible nails. The fresh air that enters the room could also help eliminate the scent inside the house if it was left unopened for quite some time, as it can be distracting for some buyers.

Keep Your Pets off the Premises

Not everyone who is going to visit your home is fond of animals. For this reason, you need to take your pets, and any hints that a pet lives in your house, somewhere else during the time that you have decided to have an open house. This can help prevent any potential trouble such as visitors having allergy attacks, your dog suddenly marking his territory, or having to scream "Down!" to your dog when he suddenly decides that visitors are not welcome in the house.

Children are Not Allowed

Make sure that your kids, no matter how well behaved and adorable they are, are not in your property during an open house. You do not want you and your buyers to be distracted when children decide to play or get food from the pantry, especially when you are about to sell your home.

Be Mindful of the Sound

Some sellers think that playing music can put on a great vibe during an open house. However, this may turn off some potential buyers. Some of them may think that you are trying to cover the noise coming from the road or the neighbor, which may actually dissuade them from buying your property. Some may also react negatively to the type of music that you are playing during the event. You may want to consider staying away from the player to avoid creating trouble.

Make All Rooms Accessible

If you were not able to stage all of your rooms, then there is no reason for you to put it yet in the market. You have to keep in mind that the open house is made for buyers to have complete access in your home and see if your property would work out for their lifestyle. Blocking people from having access to any cabinet, room, or any area in your home undermines your property and a sure way to ruin a possible sale.

Refrain from using sprays

The smell of sprays may turn off some buyers, as they believe that sprays are used to hide something unbearable (such as the sprays that are used to extinguish cockroaches or other pests). Sprays sometimes have a powerful smell, and may irritate those who have allergies.

Instead of using sprays, you can resort to using air coming from outside your home or even lighting aroma-scented candles. Not only are these relaxing, their scent is also tolerable for most people. Getting more than one sense organ stimulated and having a positive experience can influence buyers into considering your property as their new home.

Bake cookies or bread and offer it to visitors

Another way to get the buyer's sense of smell stimulated is to use food, such as the smell of baked goods like cookies and bread. It also awakens the person's sense of home, associating the smell by being at home. This could somehow reinforce the visitor to consider your property as the new place where they would want to live. This gesture can also be a way to show your buyers that they are welcomed in your home.

Be Mindful and Have Some Security

Keep in mind that you are welcoming complete strangers in your property, and you do not want any security issues in your house especially when it is still on the market. Security issues in open houses are not new – there are instances when some pose as buyers and then vandalize your property. If you think that you cannot handle security issues on your own, then it would be best to get the assistance of the neighborhood security or the local police.

Prepare your Documents

Expect prospective buyers to ask for documents about your maintenance and service warranties, blueprints for any layout changes that you have done in your property, inspection reports, and comps and appraisal. Prepare these documents in advance and make sure that you are ready to show them during open house.

Have Some Off Hours

Open house events can be tiring, especially if you are trying to sell your property on your own. Make sure that you have time for rest and for rearranging your staged house for your next set of visitors. You may want to take breaks during lunch and early afternoon. These times yield fewer visitors, and you may want to use these hours instead for catching up with personal errands, setting up your treats, and straightening your staged house from previous visits, and preparing for upcoming visitors.

These tips ensure that all of your efforts in staging your house pay off. If you were able to do all of these tips during your open house, then you will have the confidence that you will land a good deal in no time at all.

Conclusion

Thank you again for purchasing this book!

I hope this book was able to help you to stage your home properly so that more buyers will be interested into purchasing your property and make it as their own.

The next step is to apply the steps mentioned above and think of other specific techniques that you can use inside the property so you can sell it faster.

Finally, if you enjoyed this book, please take the time to share your thoughts and post a review on Amazon. We do our best to reach out to readers and provide the best value we can. Your positive review will help us achieve that. It'd be greatly appreciated!

Thank you and good luck!

CPSIA information can be obtained at www.ICGtesting.com
Printed in the USA
LVOW11s2239060715

445221LV00016B/195/P